A MAN'S
INSTRUCTION BOOK

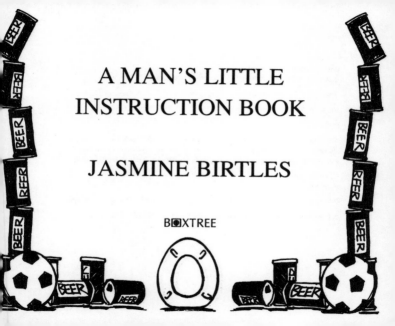

A MAN'S LITTLE
INSTRUCTION BOOK

JASMINE BIRTLES

BOXTREE

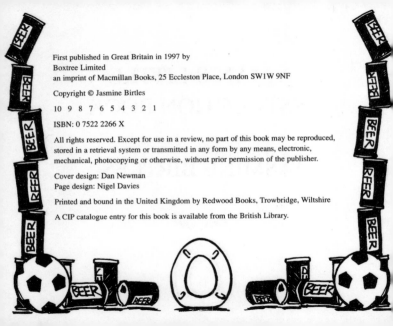

First published in Great Britain in 1997 by
Boxtree Limited
an imprint of Macmillan Books, 25 Eccleston Place, London SW1W 9NF

10 9 8 7 6 5 4 3 2 1

ISBN: 0 7522 2266 X

Cover design: Dan Newman
Page design: Nigel Davies

Printed and bound in the United Kingdom by Redwood Books, Trowbridge, Wiltshire

A CIP catalogue entry for this book is available from the British Library.

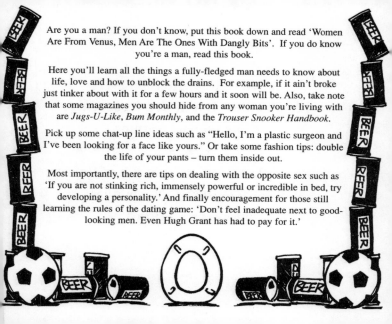

Are you a man? If you don't know, put this book down and read 'Women Are From Venus, Men Are The Ones With Dangly Bits'. If you do know you're a man, read this book.

Here you'll learn all the things a fully-fledged man needs to know about life, love and how to unblock the drains. For example, if it ain't broke just tinker about with it for a few hours and it soon will be. Also, take note that some magazines you should hide from any woman you're living with are *Jugs-U-Like*, *Bum Monthly*, and the *Trouser Snooker Handbook*.

Pick up some chat-up line ideas such as "Hello, I'm a plastic surgeon and I've been looking for a face like yours." Or take some fashion tips: double the life of your pants – turn them inside out.

Most importantly, there are tips on dealing with the opposite sex such as 'If you are not stinking rich, immensely powerful or incredible in bed, try developing a personality.' And finally encouragement for those still learning the rules of the dating game: 'Don't feel inadequate next to good-looking men. Even Hugh Grant has had to pay for it.'

Service your relationship every
12,000 miles. That'll stop it suddenly
stalling without warning.

• • •

A box of chocolates and a bunch of flowers
will solve most romantic hurdles –
unless she's a florist.

A regularly maintained relationship
is like a car – good for years of
trouble-free rides.

• • •

If your new girlfriend won't let you
have fun she's probably just practising
for when you get married.

7

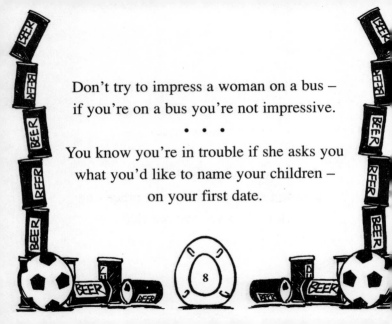

Don't try to impress a woman on a bus –
if you're on a bus you're not impressive.

• • •

You know you're in trouble if she asks you
what you'd like to name your children –
on your first date.

8

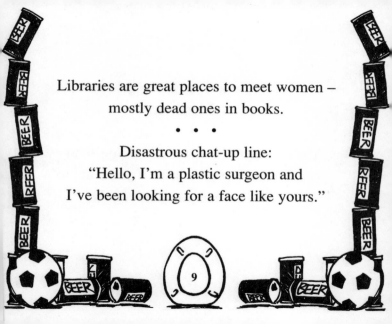

Libraries are great places to meet women –
mostly dead ones in books.

• • •

Disastrous chat-up line:
"Hello, I'm a plastic surgeon and
I've been looking for a face like yours."

9

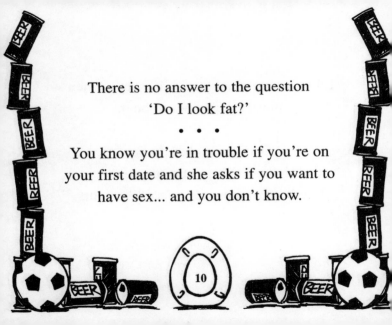

There is no answer to the question
'Do I look fat?'

• • •

You know you're in trouble if you're on
your first date and she asks if you want to
have sex... and you don't know.

10

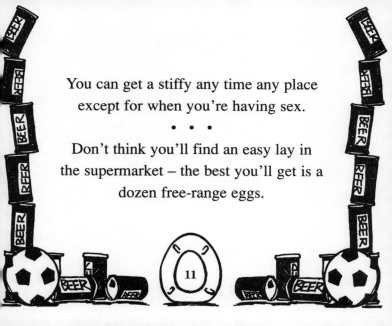

You can get a stiffy any time any place except for when you're having sex.

• • •

Don't think you'll find an easy lay in the supermarket – the best you'll get is a dozen free-range eggs.

11

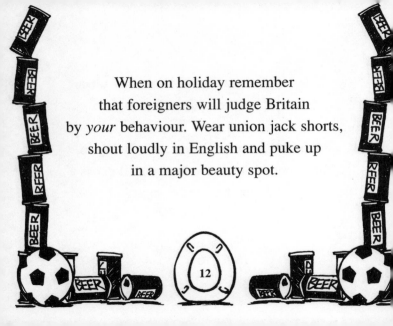

When on holiday remember
that foreigners will judge Britain
by *your* behaviour. Wear union jack shorts,
shout loudly in English and puke up
in a major beauty spot.

If you're trying to get off
with someone at work,
photocopying your genitals
and faxing them to her is bound
to impress… your friends.

Women are really impressed
by synchronised farting, loud
belching and being able to pee
your name in the snow.
(And I'm a potato.)

14

Definition of a party:
a noisy event where blokes
get pissed, try to disrobe women
and fail to direct their wee
anywhere near the toilet bowl.

Why is it that every time
you get drunk someone creeps
into your bedroom, vomits
in your shoes and pees
in your wardrobe?

If you want to meet women,
hang around outside female toilets.
Women spend half their lives queueing
for loos and they'll be grateful for
someone to relieve the boredom.

If you shake it more than twice,
you're playing with it.

• • •

If you want to chat up a woman,
shed your inhibitions, not her clothing.

18

The reason why some men
have small penises – whittling.

• • •

If you're reading this on the NET
you should stop and get yourself a life.

19

Even if you understood women
you still wouldn't believe it.

• • •

A hint: If she loves the Chippendales,
don't visit an antique shop to find out
how much they cost.

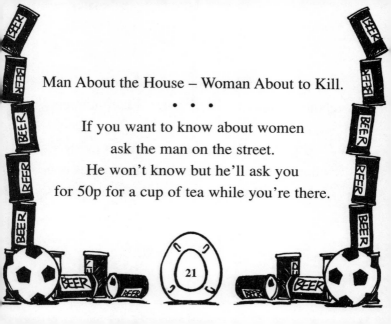

Man About the House – Woman About to Kill.

• • •

If you want to know about women
ask the man on the street.
He won't know but he'll ask you
for 50p for a cup of tea while you're there.

You know you've found a wild woman if her phone number is listed under 'Entertainment'.

• • •

If you get desperate just smile at every woman you see. By the law of averages one in a hundred is bound to show interest.

22

A man always has one tool that's special
to him – usually it's the beer bottle opener.

• • •

Avoid drinking and driving, just *pretend*
to get legless and tell everyone you're going
to steal a car on the way home.

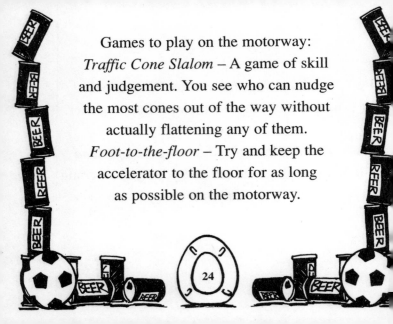

Games to play on the motorway:

Traffic Cone Slalom – A game of skill and judgement. You see who can nudge the most cones out of the way without actually flattening any of them.

Foot-to-the-floor – Try and keep the accelerator to the floor for as long as possible on the motorway.

24

Business definitions:

Over-time – Time spent doing the work you never quite got round to doing in the day.

Explanation – Lie.

Convincing explanation – Inspired lie.

A *major business venture* – One that can't be completed by dictating one letter.

Research – To look up what the last person on the project found out.

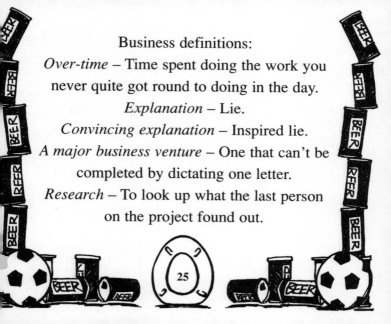

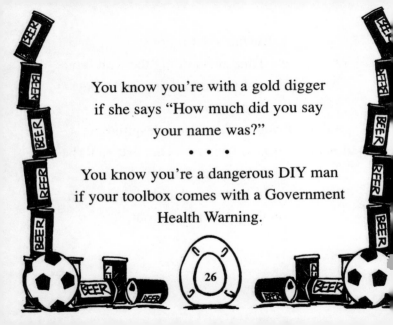

You know you're with a gold digger
if she says "How much did you say
your name was?"

• • •

You know you're a dangerous DIY man
if your toolbox comes with a Government
Health Warning.

26

Whoever said that blonds have more fun
wasn't married to Margaret Thatcher.

• • •

Even if you don't know an erogenous zone
from a parking zone you can still pull a bird
if you pretend to understand her star sign.

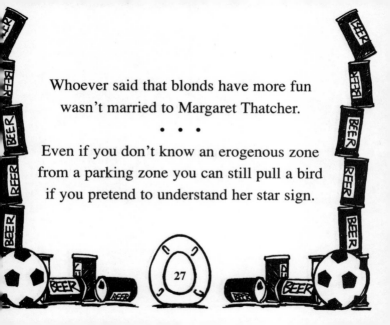

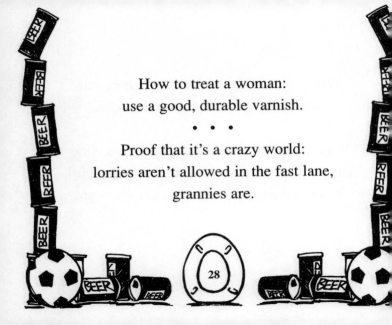

How to treat a woman:
use a good, durable varnish.

• • •

Proof that it's a crazy world:
lorries aren't allowed in the fast lane,
grannies are.

Don't eat yellow snow.

• • •

When buying a car remember
it's a scientific fact that the bigger
the tank, the higher your status and
therefore the bigger your dick.

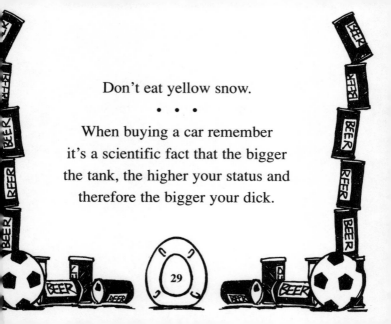

Tell a woman she's thin
and she'll do *anything* for you.

• • •

If it ain't broke just tinker about with it
for a few hours and it soon will be.

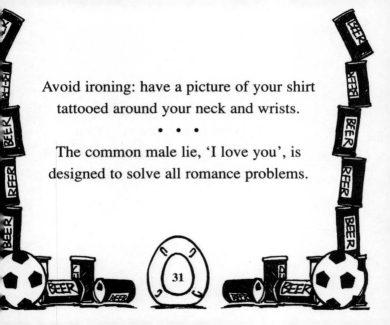

Avoid ironing: have a picture of your shirt tattooed around your neck and wrists.

• • •

The common male lie, 'I love you', is designed to solve all romance problems.

Prove to your partner that she
has a great body by taking
illicit photos of her, showing them
to all your mates and getting them
to come round and back you up.

32

If you're desperate for a woman go to a nightclub. There you can pick up women without the necessity of conversational skills, taste or personality.

Record your voice and have it
in a tape recorder under your pillow.
After sex, switch it on so
she thinks you're still
talking to her.

34

If you go out with a beautiful woman
it will be good for your ego and
will make your friends jealous –
until they find out how much
you had to pay the agency.

Try not to fart in the first
two months of any relationship.

• • •

Never criticise your boss…
to his face.

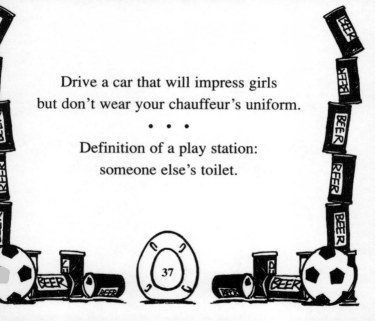

Drive a car that will impress girls
but don't wear your chauffeur's uniform.

• • •

Definition of a play station:
someone else's toilet.

Whenever you do a dump,
always tell your girlfriend about it.

• • •

People who say that money can't buy love
are the ones who can't afford it.

It's fun to tease your partner during sex –
let a little air out of the nozzle.

• • •

When women say what attracts them most to
a man is a sense of humour – they're joking.

39

You can meet a woman you fancy,
visibly slaver over her, barely contain
your lust and blurt out inane
sexist comments. Afterwards she will
still tell her friends "he's really *sweet*".

How to make love to a woman:
1) Take your hand off the TV remote control.
2) Try and remember her name.
3) Resign yourself to the fact that you won't get an action replay later on if you try and get it done in the ad break before *Match of the Day*.

A fool and his money
are soon married.

• • •

Always try to make women happy –
even if it means going out of your way
to avoid them.

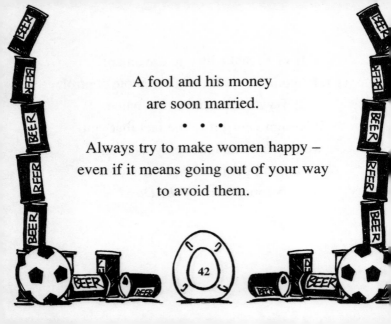

Beware of puppy love –
it can lead to a dog's life.

• • •

You know you've had too much to drink
when somebody steps on your tongue.

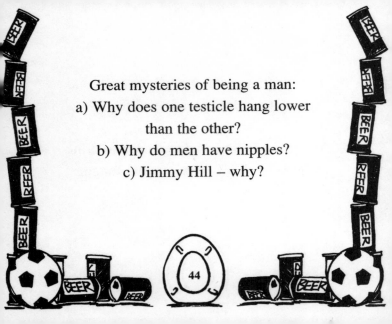

Great mysteries of being a man:
a) Why does one testicle hang lower
than the other?
b) Why do men have nipples?
c) Jimmy Hill – why?

44

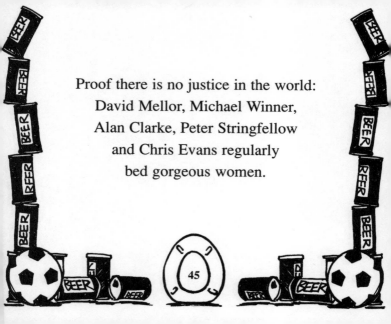

Proof there is no justice in the world:
David Mellor, Michael Winner,
Alan Clarke, Peter Stringfellow
and Chris Evans regularly
bed gorgeous women.

45

If you think that a woman who
is bright, witty, clever,
capable and attractive is
too much for you,
you're probably right.

If you can't get a woman
get a dog. They're affectionate,
forgiving and they
understand the importance
of farting.

47

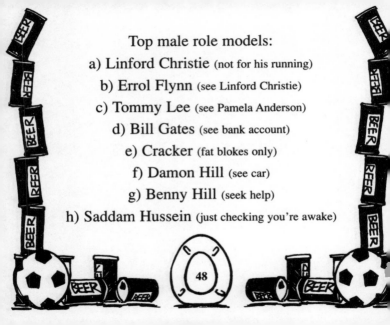

Top male role models:

a) Linford Christie (not for his running)

b) Errol Flynn (see Linford Christie)

c) Tommy Lee (see Pamela Anderson)

d) Bill Gates (see bank account)

e) Cracker (fat blokes only)

f) Damon Hill (see car)

g) Benny Hill (seek help)

h) Saddam Hussein (just checking you're awake)

Ways to be cool: a) Sleep in the fridge,
b) Never wear a vest, c) Move to Alaska.

• • •

If she has a plastic carrier bag collection,
an elastoplast on her ankle, a teddy bear
in her bedroom and she emits a kind
of whiney noise… she's a girl.

49

If you want to feel better about yourself,
try listening to phone-ins.

• • •

Never have your nails polished unless
you want to be a cross-dresser.
Then go for Flaming Scarlet.

New and improved can't beat
old and worn.

. . .

Never treat a woman like a piece of meat.
They hate it if you stick them under the grill
for ten minutes and serve them with chips.

51

Pretend you're in the SAS.
Only ever visit your girlfriend
in the dead of night, crashing
through the window wearing
a black balaclava.

Favourite female lies:
a) Size doesn't matter.
b) Of course I'm not just
interested in your money.
c) You're the best lover
I've ever had.

Confuse your girlfriend:
show an interest in her career.

• • •

Get a job handling obscene amounts
of other people's money and be
disgustingly careless with it.

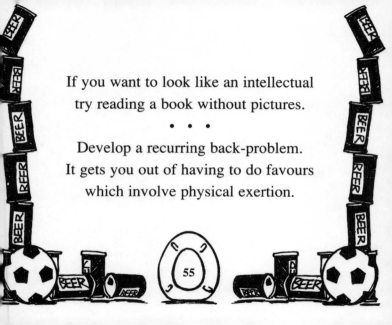

If you want to look like an intellectual
try reading a book without pictures.

• • •

Develop a recurring back-problem.
It gets you out of having to do favours
which involve physical exertion.

55

Wash vegetables well,
then chuck them out and have a burger.

• • •

If you are not stinking rich,
immensely powerful or incredible in bed,
try developing a personality.

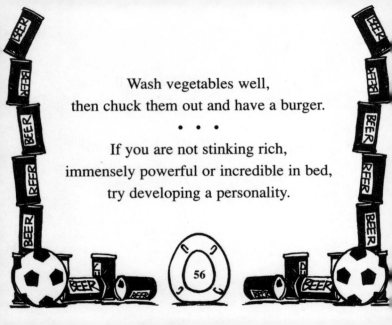

When in doubt, keep your mouth shut
and your wallet closed.

• • •

Don't take your work home –
no one sees you doing it, therefore no one's
impressed, so it's a waste of time.

57

Don't waste money on
a psychiatrist. If you need
to talk about your sad,
pathetic, inadequate personal life
become a stand-up comedian.

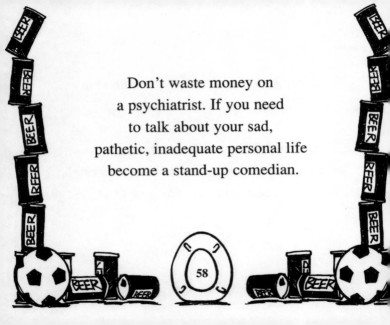

Never criticise your boss.
Put your grievances
in an anonymous press release
and fax them to the
national media.

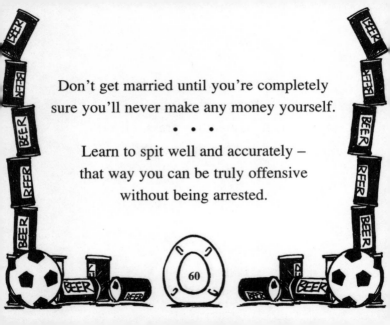

Don't get married until you're completely
sure you'll never make any money yourself.

• • •

Learn to spit well and accurately –
that way you can be truly offensive
without being arrested.

60

Retire while you're still young enough
to enjoy it. About 28 should do.

• • •

Remarkably, very few women are interested
in trainspotting, stamp collecting or DIY.
They have shoes.

Don't grow a beard.
Beards are for cissies and Noel Edmonds.

• • •

Never go to the ballet or opera unless it is
with clients, then read all the reviews
beforehand and spout them out as your
own views.

Don't accept reverse charge calls.
If your mate is in real trouble he can ring 999.

• • •

Always stop and drive after children
who throw things at your car. After all,
half the fun for them is the fear
of getting caught.

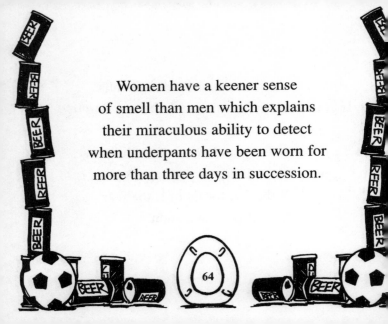

Women have a keener sense
of smell than men which explains
their miraculous ability to detect
when underpants have been worn for
more than three days in succession.

If you get bored on public transport call up your girlfriend on your mobile phone and have a loud and personal argument with her. Well, you want to keep the other passengers entertained, don't you?

How to impress at a dinner party.
Leave the Liebfraumilch-in-a-box at home.

• • •

Restrain yourself from correcting
grammatical errors made by men with
multiple tattoos and a couple
of teeth missing.

Remember, you only cheated
if you got caught.

• • •

Don't join the army –
you have to get up really early and
carry heavy things through mud.

If your girlfriend keeps you waiting
for an hour while she prepares herself
for a big night on the town,
when she finally emerges ask her
what she's going to wear.

If you're wondering what kind
of music to favour, consider the groupies:
rock music attracts Pamela Anderson,
Heather Locklear and Patsy Kensit…
need you look further?

69

Don't waste money on a
fast car to pull the birds.
Just borrow a baby – they're free,
easy to carry and women turn
to goo when they see one.

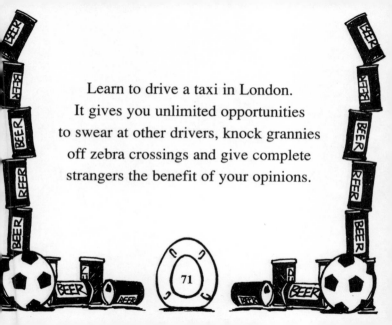

Learn to drive a taxi in London.
It gives you unlimited opportunities
to swear at other drivers, knock grannies
off zebra crossings and give complete
strangers the benefit of your opinions.

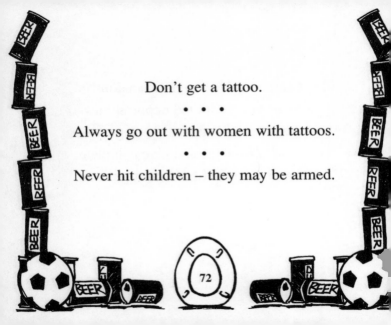

Don't get a tattoo.

• • •

Always go out with women with tattoos.

• • •

Never hit children – they may be armed.

Don't do an evening class in
cake decorating thinking you'll
find a woman. No right-thinking female
will go for a man who can
top them in sugarcraft.

A good loser is still a loser.

• • •

Sports stars are generally thick,
sports writers are thicker and sports fans
are the thickest of all.

For any one article in a
newspaper you will find another
that says exactly the opposite.
Save time.
Only look at the pictures.

75

Show respect to anyone in
a uniform, particularly security guards
as they have always learnt some
nasty tricks during their stint at
Her Majesty's Pleasure.

Learn to lie convincingly so that you can join a dating agency. Their books are always top-heavy with women but you need to fill in a form – hence the need to lie.

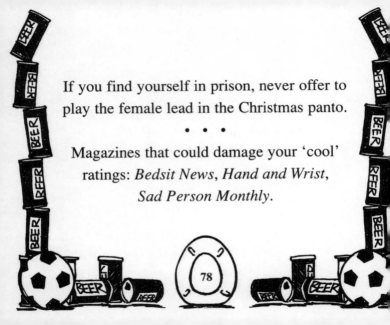

If you find yourself in prison, never offer to play the female lead in the Christmas panto.

• • •

Magazines that could damage your 'cool' ratings: *Bedsit News*, *Hand and Wrist*, *Sad Person Monthly*.

Never go in for Pyramid selling –
unless it's the kind that Fergie sits under.

• • •

Magazines you should hide from any woman
you're living with: *Jugs-U-Like*, *Bum
Monthly*, *Trouser Snooker Handbook*.

Watches that beep on the hour
every hour are called 'idiot alerts'.

• • •

If you were supposed to read between
the lines there would be words there.

80

Always do business with people who are
in a position to give the biggest bribes.

• • •

Never invest money with your in-laws.
They will rapidly become your out-laws.

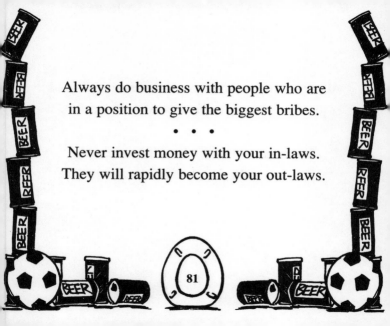

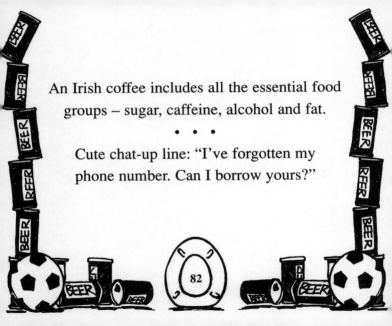

An Irish coffee includes all the essential food groups – sugar, caffeine, alcohol and fat.

• • •

Cute chat-up line: "I've forgotten my phone number. Can I borrow yours?"

Never tell secrets to anyone –
unless they're somebody else's.

• • •

If you ever feel fat and ugly just watch
International Darts.

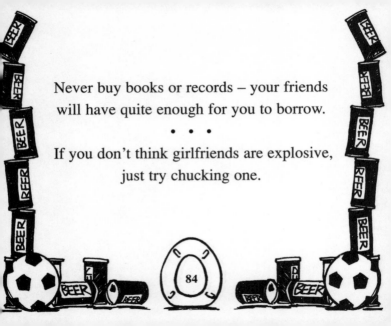

Never buy books or records – your friends
will have quite enough for you to borrow.

• • •

If you don't think girlfriends are explosive,
just try chucking one.

Show me the man who understands women
and I'll show you a man with his eyes shut.

• • •

Stop complaining.
Women are the best opposite sex you have.

A woman will never show you
her true colours until the day
she forgets her make-up.

• • •

You have to admire your boss.
If you don't you get fired.

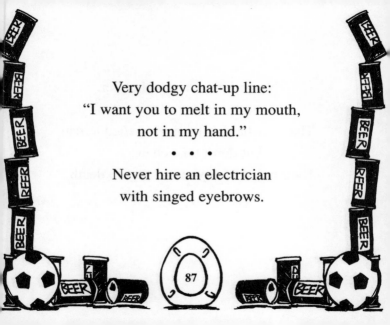

Very dodgy chat-up line:
"I want you to melt in my mouth,
not in my hand."

• • •

Never hire an electrician
with singed eyebrows.

Never hire a damp plumber.

• • •

They say hard work never killed a man
but don't take chances.
Ever heard of anyone resting to death?

Never hire a carpenter with more
than one finger missing.

• • •

If the early bird catches the worm then
stay in bed. Who needs worms?

Don't brag about being a good lover –
it won't stand up.

• • •

If you believe in working extra hours,
not cheating the company and being nice to
customers – you're the boss.

The best time to buy a used car
is when it's new.

• • •

If you think nobody cares, try missing
a couple of insurance payments.

Double the life of your pants –
turn them inside out.

• • •

Automotive law: your car will
only break down on your way home from
work – not on the way to it.

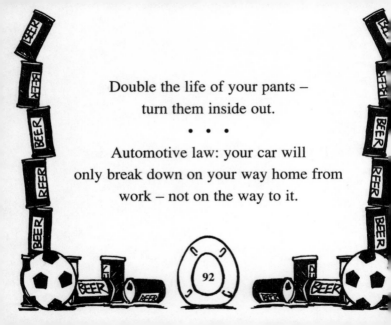

The loudest noise in the world is
the first rattle in your new car.

• • •

Don't eat greens. The colours you
should eat are brown, red and yellow,
e.g. a Big Mac and chips.

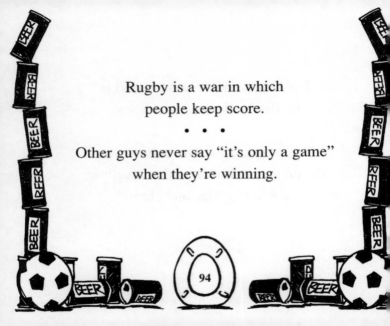

Rugby is a war in which
people keep score.

• • •

Other guys never say "it's only a game"
when they're winning.

94

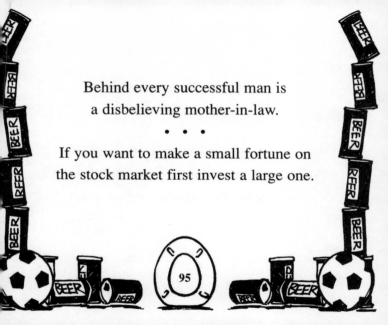

Behind every successful man is
a disbelieving mother-in-law.

• • •

If you want to make a small fortune on
the stock market first invest a large one.

Talk is cheap unless
you're a lawyer.

• • •

Ridiculous chat up line:
"You've got everything a man could want...
a moustache, big muscles, a beer gut..."

Don't waste money on vet's bills.
Just get another cat – it's cheaper.

• • •

You can be pretty sure you're not the
only man in her life if her phone number
is listed under 'Leisure'.

If you don't do something completely
crazy every now and then you'll go mad.

• • •

If you want to look attractive hang around
with really ugly blokes.

If you want to get talking to a girl in a bar,
steal her drink.

• • •

Always aim high –
that way you won't splash your shoes.

It is better to give than to receive –
particularly if you're in a boxing ring.

• • •

Do unto others before
they do it unto you.

100

A hair in the head is worth
two combed over.

• • •

Never hit a man when he's down.
Kick him, it's much easier.

Join Alcoholics Anonymous –
you can still drink but under an
assumed name.

• • •

In a urinal don't flatter yourself.
Stand closer.

If you need to feel wanted,
rob some banks.

• • •

Many women only fall for men who
treat them badly. So act like a shit and
see those women rush to you.

Become a lawyer. Make crime pay.

• • •

If you're on a first date, it is
inadvisable immediately to rip all
your clothes off and ask her if
she'd like a delivery of salami.

Don't feel inadequate next to
good-looking men.
Even Hugh Grant has had to pay for it.

• • •

If you can't hook a woman by your looks,
position and personality, try a fishing rod.

Recommended habits to indulge in
while you're still single (cos you won't
get the chance once you're hitched):
1) unlimited flatulence,
2) always keeping the toilet seat up
even when doing a dump,

3) practising resonant choral belching every day,
4) thinking that flushing the toilet is
the same as cleaning it,
5) decorating your flat with pizza boxes,
lager cans and traffic cones on a seething and
pulsating bed of old pants.

Bra fastenings are made by the
same people who make bank vaults.

• • •

You're a new man if you're always looking
for a meaningful one-night stand.

As a first date, avoid taking her
to the Cup Final.

• • •

To get really in with her,
find out what her favourite flower is.
If she says self-raising, give up.

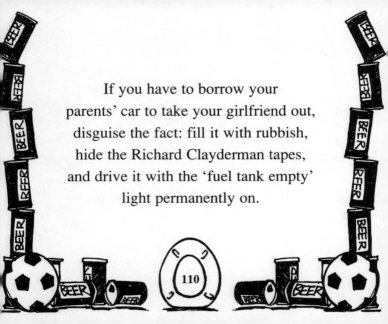

If you have to borrow your
parents' car to take your girlfriend out,
disguise the fact: fill it with rubbish,
hide the Richard Clayderman tapes,
and drive it with the 'fuel tank empty'
light permanently on.

Ensure extra room for yourself
on public transport by washing
only once a week, singing loudly
and carrying a well-thumbed copy of
Fetish Fanatic's Digest.

Don't bother going to high street
stores to buy hi-fi equipment.
You can buy the same items cheaper
in many old pubs in the
less pricey parts of town.

It's now possible to buy
'female attracting' scents.
The most successful is a bottle of
'I'm A Multimillionaire With
Two Weeks To Live' cologne.

Impress women by
performing fiveplay.

• • •

Topics you should avoid when
chatting up: farting, your toilet habits,
your last operation, football,
sport of any kind, your wife.

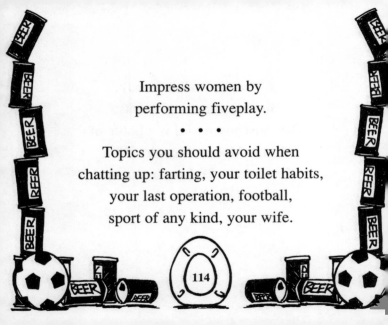

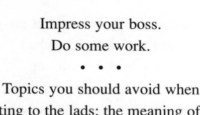

Impress your boss.
Do some work.

• • •

Topics you should avoid when
chatting to the lads: the meaning of life,
God, crochet, cookery tips, relationships,
your impotence.

115

You can try if you like, but no one
has yet found a way in which they
can drink for a living.

• • •

Don't bother going to the ballet.
You can never tell which side is winning.

Don't go looking for a wife.
Go out with single women.

• • •

When you're behind the wheel
beware of children.
They're terrible drivers.

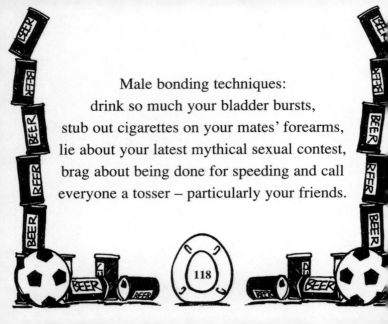

Male bonding techniques:
drink so much your bladder bursts,
stub out cigarettes on your mates' forearms,
lie about your latest mythical sexual contest,
brag about being done for speeding and call
everyone a tosser – particularly your friends.

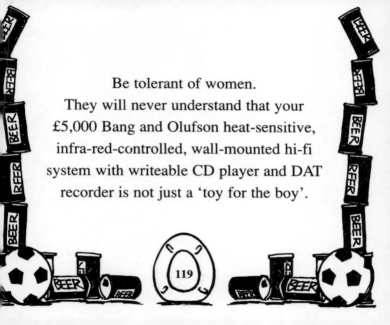

Be tolerant of women.
They will never understand that your
£5,000 Bang and Olufson heat-sensitive,
infra-red-controlled, wall-mounted hi-fi
system with writeable CD player and DAT
recorder is not just a 'toy for the boy'.

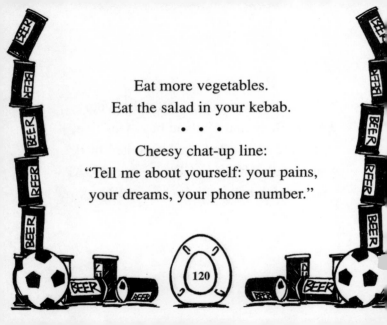

Eat more vegetables.
Eat the salad in your kebab.

• • •

Cheesy chat-up line:
"Tell me about yourself: your pains,
your dreams, your phone number."

120

Never flirt with the wife
of a hitman.

• • •

Ignore relationship problems.
If you wait for long enough she'll do
something about them.

121

Don't believe people who tell you
swimming is the best exercise.
Have you seen the shape of a whale?

• • •

If you live on your own,
remember there are three basic food groups:
tinned, frozen and take-away.

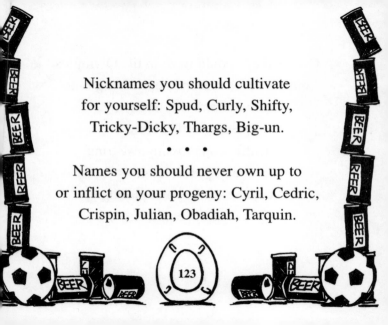

Nicknames you should cultivate for yourself: Spud, Curly, Shifty, Tricky-Dicky, Thargs, Big-un.

• • •

Names you should never own up to or inflict on your progeny: Cyril, Cedric, Crispin, Julian, Obadiah, Tarquin.

123

Events they should have in the Olympics
but for some reason keep leaving out:
1) Synchronised moonying,
2) Beer bottle skittles,
3) Traffic cone tossing, wearing
and positioning,
4) Gnome stealing and placing in
suggestive poses,

124

5) Undoing a bra in under ten hours,
6) Chatting up the ugliest bird in the pub
then dumping her.

• • •

Croquet is not a good sport to support.
It is played by toffee-nosed girls and men
with no chins and does not
inspire hooliganism.

Never use the maps in the
glove compartment or ask for directions,
even if the last habitation you passed looked
uncannily like an igloo and the scenery has
become remarkably white.

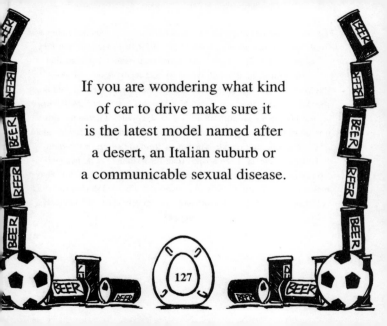

If you are wondering what kind
of car to drive make sure it
is the latest model named after
a desert, an Italian suburb or
a communicable sexual disease.

Jasmine Birtles has had a lot of contact with men – even her father was one. She has provided an opening for all of Boyzone (not that they were interested) and she has worked under several famous and powerful men, although if you try and report it she will sue.

She likes to think that she's in touch with her masculine side, although she doesn't have to shave as often as Vanessa Feltz. In fact, she once tried being a man but failed because she couldn't name the full line-up of the winning team in the 1953 cup final. As an Independent she also couldn't decide whether to dress to the left or the right. However, she has been a consultant for Man at C & A, her main piece of advice being "The escalators are over there, sir." She also masterminded Robin Cook's successful use of tweed during the 1997 elections. She lives in Norfolk and has a matching set of twins and a talking piglet.